National Research and Development Centre
for adult literacy and numeracy

Models of
adult learning:
a literature review

Karin Tusting and David Barton

niace

promoting adult learning

Published by the National Institute of Adult Continuing Education
(England and Wales) 2006, Reprinted 2008

21 De Montfort Street
Leicester LE1 7GE
Company registration no. 2603322
Charity registration no. 1002775

First published by the National Research and Development Centre for Adult
Literacy and Numeracy 2003

promoting adult learning

NIACE has a broad remit to promote lifelong learning opportunities for
adults. NIACE works to develop increased participation in education and
training, particularly for those who do not have easy access because of barriers of class, gender, age, race, language and culture, learning difficulties
and disabilities, or insufficient financial resources.

NIACE's website is www.niace.org.uk

Cataloguing in Publication Data
A CIP record of this title is available from the British Library

ISBN 978 1 86201 280 6

Designed and typeset by Prestige Filmsetters
Printed in the UK by Latimer Trend

1084120
£9.95

CONTENTS

Page

Preface

This book was originally published as a research review by the National Research and Development Centre for Adult Literacy and Numeracy (NRDC). The work was funded by the Department for Education and Skills in England as part of **Skills for Life**: the national strategy for improving adult literacy and numeracy skills. The original NRDC project was directed by David Barton and Diana Coben and we are grateful to Diana Coben and Rachel Hodge for detailed comments on earlier drafts of the original review.

We are pleased that the review can now reach a wider audience, both of people working in adult language, literacy and numeracy, and also in the field of adult learning more generally.

The views expressed are ours, as authors, and do not necessarily reflect those of the Department for Education and Skills.

Karin Tusting and *David Barton*.

Summary

Ideas about what learning is and how it is achieved are central to all aspects of adult learning, including work in adult basic skills. Theories of learning provide a starting point for principles of teaching. Any curriculum or training course has views of learning built into it and any teaching plan is based upon a view of how people learn.

Most educational research is on children and most views of learning have been developed in the context of children learning within a formal educational system. Inevitably such views have been tied into child development and compulsory schooling. In contrast, this book is a review of models of learning that have focused on adults. It is a wide-ranging review and covers ideas from many fields about how adults learn: the aim is to provide ideas that are useful for research into teaching and learning. The theories covered are ones that have proved useful in relation to the education of adults.

The adult research began as a reaction to child-based models and aimed to sketch out the distinctiveness of adult learning, developing an adult-based androgogy to be contrasted with child-based pedagogy. This work has shifted to recognise that there are different types of learning and that different models of learning are appropriate to different situations. These models point to the richness and complexity of learning and, rather than seeing them as right or wrong, we aim to show how they contribute to one another and add to the understanding of learning. They are presented here as providing potential for use in adult learning.

The key ideas about how adults learn are that:

1. Adults have their own motivations for learning. Learners build on their existing knowledge and experience. They fit learning into their own purposes and become engaged in it. People's purposes for learning are

related to their real lives and the practices and roles they engage in outside the classroom.

2. Adults have a drive towards self-direction and towards becoming autonomous learners. Learning is initiated by the learner and one role of the teacher is to provide a secure environment in which learning can take place.

3. Adults have the ability to learn about their own learning processes, and can benefit from discussion and reflection on this. They are able to learn how to learn. For instance, there are different learning styles that people synthesise. Teaching can enable learners to develop their range of learning styles.

4. Learning is a characteristic of all real-life activities, in which people take on different roles and participate in different ways. People learn by engaging in practice and their participation can be supported in new ways. Teaching can 'scaffold' these activities, enabling learners to develop new forms of expertise.

5. Adults reflect and build upon their experience. Reflective learning is generated when people encounter problems and issues in their real lives and think about ways of resolving them.

6. Reflective learning is unique to each person, since it arises out of the complexities of their own experience. A great deal of learning is incidental and idiosyncratically related to the learner: it cannot be planned in advance. While there are things that can be done to encourage reflective experiential learning, there is no set of steps that can be followed to guarantee it will happen.

7. Reflective learning enables people to reorganise experience and 'see' situations in new ways. In this way, adult learning is potentially transformative, both personally and socially.

Introduction

This book summarises a wide-ranging review of literature on adult learning, drawing out the different models of adult learning and their significance for research and development in adult language, literacy and numeracy. Most research in learning has focused primarily on children, and most views of learning have been developed within the context of children being educated in a formal school system. However, when one moves away from models of child development, and examines the models produced from disciplines looking at settings beyond compulsory schooling, a very different view of learning emerges. The aim of this review is to survey these fields and thereby provide useful ideas for developing teaching and learning for adults.

Historically, the field that has addressed learning most directly is psychology. Early theories developed in the USA and Europe saw learning principally as a phenomenon of the individual. This review outlines the principal features of these theories, focusing on behaviourism, cognitivism, cognitive constructivism and developmental psychology. At the same time, within the fields of sociocultural psychology, activity theory and situated cognition, work in the Soviet Union developed understandings of learning as a form of social participation, and this has been followed by more recent research in Europe and the US that takes the same approach. We summarise the main features of this body of work.

In outlining these approaches, we bring to light two distinct paradigms of learning in psychology: that which sees learning as principally concerning processes going on within an individual, and a more recent one which understands learning as being a socially situated phenomenon, best described and understood in terms of people's ongoing participation in social contexts and interaction. Brain science has seen a similar shift: from theories that focused on the development and characteristics of the brain as an isolated entity to more recent understandings of the brain as developing in a fundamentally interactive way with the world around it. We therefore also briefly mention developments in this field.

Adult education is of course another significant area in which theories of adult learning have been developed. Much of the literature in this field is driven by the question of whether or not there are features of adult learning that make adult education a field of work and enquiry in itself, separate from the discipline of studying learning in schools. We begin by considering models that have taken this starting point, describing the characteristics of learning that have been identified as being 'distinctive' to adults. Several of these features have become significant fields of theory in their own right.

One key idea within the field of adult learning theory is the model of the adult as a self-directed or autonomous learner. Any model of adult learning that claims to be complete has to take into account the self-directedness of much learning, and the fact that the majority of learning in people's lives takes place outside formal learning provision. We present a summary of work on self-directed learning, informal learning and learning how to learn. Another influential idea in the field has been that adults learn primarily through reflection on their experience. We briefly present the ideas of the primary theorists in the field of reflective and experiential learning. Critical reflection is often central to those models of adult learning which see learning as individually and/or socially transformative, and these transformative models will be described. We also examine the claims made by theorists taking a postmodern approach to learning.

We move on to address models of learning produced from other fields. It is often said that we live in a context of continual, rapid and unprecedented change, and that this is one of the reasons why adult learning has become increasingly important. We examine models of learning developed in two fields that address this question of change directly: management learning, and online and distance learning.

We conclude by summarising the main findings of the review and suggest that a full understanding of adult learning must be a complex one. Rather than seeing learning principally as an individual, cognitive phenomenon, it must take into account the interrelationship of the many factors in the learning situation, and place the learner's contexts, purposes and practices at the centre. We also list the implications of the review for our understanding of adults' learning.

Models from psychology

Behaviourism

The first significant psychological theories of learning were developed within the field of behaviourism. Coming from a paradigm that limited scientific study only to those things which could be observed directly, behaviourist psychologists avoided using any internal 'mentalist' concepts, such as thought, to explain behaviour. They restricted their explanations to those material parts of the situation that could be seen and described. Their explanations for human behaviour were therefore expressed purely in terms of conditioned responses to environmental stimuli.

The best-known theory of learning and instruction to emerge from this field is Skinner's 'operant conditioning' (see Skinner 1974 for a summary of his work). This approach uses reinforcement to shape changes in behaviour gradually, by breaking down a complex behaviour into a series of much smaller steps, and immediately rewarding any change in the desired direction. The learner then tends to repeat this behaviour, thus operating on their own environment in order to elicit more positive reinforcement.

Variants of this approach have been used to address problem behaviours such as smoking, weight gain, drug use and phobias, through 'behaviour modification' programmes. It has also formed the basis of a number of instructional models. These tend to see the role of the teacher as primarily one of 'delivering' or 'transmitting' learning by breaking complex learning down into smaller, simpler tasks. These tasks are practised repeatedly, and students are rewarded for correct completion. Pre-determined learning outcomes, phrased purely in terms of observable behaviours, are set at the start of a course or session. Behaviour that approximates to these outcomes can then be measured and rewarded.

Behaviourist models of learning offer simplicity, control, a method for approaching the teaching of complex behaviours in relatively straightforward ways, a way of measuring whether this has been achieved, and an attractive appearance of scientific rigour. However, in considering the potential for their application to adult language, literacy and numeracy provision, they have significant weaknesses. The behaviourist paradigm is concerned only with physical, observable behaviours so that the mental processes of understanding and making sense of things are beyond its remit. While it may be useful for the small sub-set of desired learning outcomes that do not require the learner to experience changed understandings in order to change behaviour patterns, it is not enough to draw on in helping people who want to learn to read, write and do maths. These are complex practices that bring together observable behaviour with non-observable understandings and beliefs.

Behaviourist models of learning imply that it may be possible to 'train' learners' responses by using behavioural techniques, breaking complex behaviours down into simple chains and rewarding correct performance. However this model can offer little to help conceptualise learners' developing understandings or autonomy.

Cognitivism

The first attempt to address this weakness in psychological theories of learning came with the development of cognitivist models, which acknowledged the limitations of seeing learning purely in terms of stimulus response and behaviour change. Instead, cognitivist approaches studied the roles of individual, internal, information-processing elements of learning. The roots of cognitivist approaches to learning can be traced back to Gestalt psychology, which drew attention to the significance of questions of perception, insight and meaning. In particular, it identified the importance of moments when learning reorganises experience so that the learner suddenly 'sees' the whole phenomenon under study in a new way.

Cognitivism rejects the model that sees learning only as changes in observable behaviour, and instead understands learning as consisting of changes in mental constructs and processes, the development and increasing sophistication of 'mental maps' and 'schemata' for representing the world. Since these processes are not directly observable, the development of theory often proceeds by making inferences about these internal cognitive processes, primarily by setting up laboratory experiments designed to be interpretable in these terms.

Work from within behaviourism began to perceive the significance of cognition in the social setting for learning. Miller and Dollard's work in the 1940s (Miller and Dollard 1941) demonstrated how reinforcement occurred not only when the subject themselves received a reward, but also when they observed another subject experiencing a stimulus-reward pattern. This proved that internal (and therefore unobservable) factors had a part to play in the learning process. This work influenced Bandura's (1977) development of a 'social learning theory'. While rooted in the behaviourist paradigm, this acknowledged the existence of observational learning and drew attention to vicarious, symbolic and self-regulatory processes that are not directly observable.

Cognitivist theorists include Gagné (see, for example, Gagné 1985), who developed a model in which learning is primarily about information processing. Gagné's theory of instruction is based on a taxonomy of learning outcomes and he suggests that particular conditions are necessary to achieve these different learning outcomes. This includes both those internal to the learner, such as the skills and capacities the learner has already mastered, and those external to the learner, such as the conditions arranged by the teacher or facilitator. He studied the conditions under which successful learning occurs, and tried to describe these objectively so that they could be replicated in other instructional settings.

For Gagné, learning is progressive in that learners draw on previously-learned skills and capacities when learning new material. He therefore states that in order to attain a particular learning outcome, such as mastery of a task, it is necessary to produce a 'learning hierarchy', by breaking the task into its more basic component skills. The teacher guides the learner through nine steps or 'events of instruction' to ascend the learning hierarchy: gaining attention (reception); informing learners of the objective (expectancy); stimulating recall of prior learning (retrieval); presenting the stimulus (selective perception); providing learning guidance (semantic encoding); eliciting performance (responding); providing feedback (reinforcement); assessing performance (retrieval); and enhancing retention and transfer (generalisation).

The roots of Gagné's thinking in behaviourism are clear, both in his terminology and in the 'chaining' structure he describes. However his focus on internal information processing, rather than externally observed behaviour, places him in the realms of the cognitivists. His work has been particularly influential in the US where his ideas have been taken up by the military and the educational establishment.

Others have also developed theories of instruction based on cognitivist under-standings of how the mind works. Ausubel's (1963) theory of instruction states that, in order for meaningful learning to take place in a context of expository instruction in school-type settings, new information needs to fit in with existing cognitive structures. He suggests the use of 'advance organisers' when presenting new material, to organise the material at a higher level of generality and abstraction before it is progressively differentiated in detail and specificity.

Cognitivist models of learning moved psychology on from the reduction-ism of the behaviourist approaches to a better understanding of the mental complexities associated with learning. The important implica-tions of these models for adult learning lie in the importance of building on learners' existing knowledge, and in the need to find ways to ensure that learners have understood or made sense of what they are learning, rather than simply focusing on eliciting the required per-formances.

Cognitive constructivism

Despite the shift in focus from seeing learning as changes in observable behaviour to seeing learning as developing internal information-processing mechanisms and models, purely cognitivist models of learning were still predicated on the notion that learning was a matter of finding ways to assim-ilate 'objective' knowledge. The next step in developing understanding was when theorists became aware that learners themselves played an active role: not merely in assimilating but also, and more importantly, in constructing the things that they were learning. While cognitivist models of learning focus on learners developing representational models of knowledge provided to them by their environment, cognitive constructivism shifts the focus to the learner's own process of actively constructing these models through interaction with their environment.

Many of these are inspired by Piaget's (1950; 1970) developmental model of learning. On the basis of long-term, detailed observation of children's development, Piaget suggested that a child's cognitive structure develops through a series of distinct stages. His significant contribution was in drawing attention to the active role of children themselves in this process. He demon-strated that, rather than simply undergoing an inevitable maturing process, children's development occurs through their active interaction with the environment in different ways.

Cognitive constructivism started from this understanding of child development and applied it to all learners, examining learners' participation in the learning process through the active construction of new models, engaging in new experiences and thereby building on and extending their existing schemata. Learning becomes an active process: not the accumulation of 'truth' or 'knowledge', but an ongoing dynamic of personal construction of meaning.

Cognitive constructivist theories of instruction reflect this understanding. For example, this is the principle behind Bruner's (1960, 1977) 'spiral curriculum'. Bruner suggests that the basic principles of any subject can be grasped very early on in its study, if the learner is helped to discover the underlying cognitive structure of the subject in a way that both fires their imagination and fits in with their existing modes of thinking. Thereafter, their learning proceeds by rearranging new evidence in a meaningful way within these existing basic structures. The role of the educator is to present new material and experiences in a way that facilitates this process; but it is the learners themselves who construct their own learning.

In terms of adult learning, cognitive constructivist theories would suggest that it is important to allow learners the choice and autonomy to develop their learning in their own way, by giving them space to follow their own individual interests and understandings, and by recognising that this process will be different for each learner.

Developmental theories

Since learning is often related to developmental processes, the field of developmental psychology has also proved influential within adult education. Many theories of human development understand humans as developing in a series of stages, and suggest that the sorts of learning that occur and the forms of instruction that are most appropriate are qualitatively different in each of these stages.

Perhaps the best known and most influential of these stage theories of development is Piaget's cognitive theory of child development, mentioned above. In this model, children pass through four stages of cognitive development, each associated with different forms of cognitive structuring, reaching a final 'formal-operational' stage in their teens which marks the first time they are able to deal with abstract logic.

Piaget's model has been very influential within education, but has also been criticised. One of the reasons is that a 'privileging' of formal abstract thought is implicit in the four-stage theory. While this is very common in

Euro-American cultures, it is becoming increasingly clear that abstract thought is only one of many modes of thinking, and is not necessarily the most powerful or appropriate in every situation (see sections on situated cognition and experiential learning for more on this). Piaget's model has therefore been seen as limited and culturally-specific and, of course, it applies principally to children.

However, the basic idea that there are stages of cognitive development has also been applied in several different ways within the context of adult education. (Merriam and Caffarella (1998) contains a good review of such work.) Perry's (1970) study, based on work with college students, suggests that undergraduates' thought processes typically develop along a continuum of nine positions, from absolutism through relativism to contextualised reasoning. Similarly, King and Kitchener (1994) identify seven stages in the process of developing reflective judgement. Belenky *et al*'s influential study, 'Women's Ways of Knowing' (1986), is again based on work in academic institutions but also used research with women in parenting classes. It suggests that women's thought develops in five stages, from silence, through received knowledge, subjective knowledge and procedural knowledge, to constructed knowledge.

Baxter Magolda's work (1992) followed a group of male and female college students over five years, interviewing them yearly. It identifies a progression in developing epistemological reflection from absolute, through transitional and independent, to contextual forms of reasoning. Kohlberg's work (1981; 1984) focused on moral development, claiming that there are six phases of moral development through which people must pass, from pre-conventional ideas of obedience and punishment, through conventional morality concerned with gaining the approval of others and following laws, to post-conventional morality which, in its most developed form, is guided by principles and conscience. Many of these stage theories appear to be describing a similar process in which learners move from absolute theories of what is right and wrong, through a stage of relativising and subjectivising everything, to a final stage where they accept the contextual and situated nature of knowledge. At this final stage, the search for truth is inflected by an awareness of the inevitability of alternative points of view and the inherent contradictions and uncertainties of real life (see also Brookfield 2000 for a characterisation of adult thinking in similar terms). While this is clearly a model that reflects the complex nature of everyday cognition more clearly than Piaget's 'formal-operational' stage, there are also questions to be raised about it. Many of these studies are based on work with small samples of college students undergoing training in a particular kind of thinking, and therefore it is doubtful whether this work can be generalised to adults as a whole.

Some theories of development identify a small number of discrete cognitive stages that people supposedly pass through in a relatively linear fashion. However, many of these models were developed through researching small samples of particular sorts of learners, often college students, so we cannot assume that they can be directly applied to all adult learners. And there is little evidence to suggest that adults' needs with regard to language, literacy, numeracy are necessarily related to any more generalised stage of cognitive development. Whereas cognitive developmental models imply a fairly reductionist, linear process of progress, we know that adult learners typically exhibit 'spiky profiles', that is to say, varying levels of ability and confidence, even within different elements of literacy and numeracy practices. This 'spikiness' is likely to extend to their lives as a whole.

Other theories of development in adulthood focus more on the significance of the different stages, phases, tasks and roles that adults engage in in social life, and the impact of these on their learning processes. One such early study was by Levinson *et al* (1978) involving the study of forty males using biographical interviews. Levinson developed a theory of a life cycle consisting of four eras, each lasting approximately 25 years, with each era having a distinctive character and period of development, and a transitional stage between each. Erikson's life-stage model similarly maps a series of stages through which people are supposed to pass, and suggests that within each there is a 'teachable moment' at which learning appropriate to that particular stage of development can happen (Erikson 1963; 1978; 1982; Erikson *et al* 1986).

Again, these models of development suggest a single linear path through which everyone is expected to progress. This absolutist thinking has been questioned by theorists who suggest that similarities in people's development are more likely to relate to the contexts, cultures and communities within which they grow, than to development understood as a phenomenon which acts in the same way irrespective of context.

Neugarten (1976) points out that every society has expectations about age-appropriate behaviour, but these differ from one society to another and are socially constructed rather than absolute. She argues that when life changes occur in a different order from that which society expects, they are experienced as problematic. Riegel (1976) develops a more complex understanding of human development as consisting of at least four dimensions: inner-biological, individual-psychological, cultural-psychological, and outer physical. He argues that periods of equilibrium between these dimensions are the exception rather than the rule. He suggests that when any two (or more) of these dimensions are in conflict, there is potential for change, and that development is therefore normally an ongoing, continual process.

Tennant and Pogson (1995) explore the significance of this development literature for adult education practice. They argue that more recent work moves beyond stage theories and comes to understand that adults develop through having the experience of dealing with real-life problems, rather than as an inevitable progression through a pre-ordained series of stages. The problems adults encounter in the real world are often not the kind which can be addressed by formal-operational logic. They tend to be open-ended, contradictory and ambiguous. They seldom have a single logical or correct solution, but nevertheless require a commitment to a single course of action such as buying one house or choosing one job from among several possibilities. This sort of problem is not 'solved', but is 'resolved' in an ongoing process. Tennant and Pogson claim that, as a result of experiencing this type of problem, adults develop a form of reasoning that they call 'dialectical thinking', in which working through the formal logical properties of a task becomes less important than the ability to draw on one's accumulation of experience in dealing with similar problems.

Tennant and Pogson suggest that notions of fixed phases and stages and ideal end-points should be abandoned, with the focus shifting to processes of change and transformation and the learning involved in these, acknowledging the multiple and non-linear pathways through which adults tend to pass. (They cite Merriam and Clark's (1991) 'Lifelines' study of work, love and learning as one which takes this perspective.) This changes the focus from normative life stages to the social and cultural processes that trigger changes and developments. It involves (but is not limited to) understanding the socially-prescribed life course patterns in different historical, social and cultural settings, as well as paying attention to psychological development. By acknowledging the social and historical dimension of development, adult educators can try to distinguish changes and learning experiences that genuinely transform and liberate from those that merely key into socially-approved life course expectations.

The implications of developmental models of adult learning are that we should not see development in adulthood as a single linear process with fixed goals towards which we are trying to move people. We must understand that many of these theories of development are socially and culturally contingent. Rather than trying to impose a single model of development, we need to know learners' current social roles and positions and the practices they engage in, and come to an understanding of the role of language, literacy and numeracy within these. This should enable us to teach in a way that enriches learners' current lives and encourages them to develop further in their desired direction.

Activity theory and social constructivism

The Soviet school of sociocultural theory or activity theory (Vygotsky 1962; 1978; Wertsch 1985a; 1985b; 1991) offers a different focus, bringing together theories of development and a constructivist approach. This was an attempt to develop a different form of psychology from the behaviourist understandings that were predominant at the time. Rather than studying behaviour in a decontextualised way, this new form of psychology examined how the human mind develops in the context of ongoing, meaningful, goal-oriented action and interaction with other people, mediated by semiotic and material tools.

Vygotsky was interested in the emergence of higher mental functioning in human beings. He therefore made developmental analysis the foundation for his study of mind (Wertsch 1985b; 1991). On the basis of a series of rigorous experimental observations, Vygotsky concluded that the development of higher mental functioning in the individual, while dependent on and rooted in biophysical processes such as the maturation of the brain, derives essentially from social interaction. Without this social interaction, higher mental functioning would not emerge. His main aim was to specify the processes involved in this.

Whereas Piaget's work developed a form of cognitive constructivism, Vygotsky is generally seen as taking a social constructivist approach. From this perspective, interaction with other people and cultural artefacts, not just with new ideas, is crucial for learning. His 'general genetic law of cultural development' claimed that any function in the child's cognitive development must first appear on the social plane, that is in interaction with others, and only thereafter on the psychological plane.

While acknowledging that the internalisation of the process changes its nature, Vygotsky claimed that the specific structures and processes of intramental functioning can always be traced to their intermental precursors. Therefore, social relations underlie the development and learning of all higher cognitive functioning. This leads to an understanding of higher mental functions, such as thinking, voluntary attention and logical memory, as being potentially social as well as individual activities. An example would be when two people 'remember something together', prompting or 'scaffolding' one another until recall is achieved.

Learning is also seen as involving this scaffolding process (Bruner 1985), particularly as it is involved in perhaps the best-known of Vygotsky's concepts in the educational field, the ZPD or Zone of Proximal Development. This refers to the difference between a learner's current level, as determined by independent problem solving, and the higher level of their potential for development, as determined through problem solving under guidance, or in collaboration with peers (Vygotsky 1978).

Vygotsky's work also draws attention to the role of mediating tools or artefacts, both material and non-material, in this interactional process. People's interactions draw on concepts, strategies, and technologies, including writing and other representational technologies, which mediate the meanings constructed. Vygotsky and colleagues showed the significance of such mediational artefacts through a series of experiments with children and with adults with impairments such as Parkinson's disease. These demonstrated that very simple mediational tools, such as coloured cards or paper templates, enabled people to perform tasks they could not otherwise do (Vygotsky 1978). Vygotsky's work supports not merely a social, but a sociocultural theory of learning, which sees cognition as distributed both between the people present in the interaction, and across such mediating 'tools for thinking' as are present in the culture more generally.

This is clearly a very different understanding from that developed by the cognitivist model described above. Rather than focusing on the role of the individual actor in constructing meaning, Vygotsky's sociocultural theory has interaction with other people at its very core.

A sociocultural understanding suggests that in adult learning, learners need interaction with others at the right level for their own stage of development, and that appropriate mediational tools and artefacts play a crucial role in the learning process.

Activity theory was further developed by Vygotsky's associates Leont'ev (1978; 1981) and Luria (1976; 1978). Translations of these writers into English in the 1970s led to their ideas being taken up by researchers in the West who developed the potential offered by understandings of human action and learning in terms of activity systems: that is, as communities of people engaging in a common activity. Studies of learning in activity systems draw our attention to the role of interaction and mediational artefacts (both material and semiotic) in goal-oriented activity, developing a very different sort of understanding from the much more individualistic cognitivist or behavioural models.

Activity theory has been developed more recently in psychology through the works of Cole, Engeström, Scribner and colleagues. A good summary of the work in this field can be found in Cole, Engeström and Vasquez' 'Mind, Culture and Activity' (1997), which draws together seminal papers from the 'Quarterly Newsletter of the Laboratory of Comparative Human Cognition'. This collection shows the historical development of an approach that studies the actions of people participating in routine, culturally-organised activities. It generates a psychology that places context, rather than individual cognition, at the centre of our understanding of human thought and activity.

Situated cognition

When psychologists began to look at how cognition occurs in real situations rather than in decontextualised laboratory settings, a situated model of learning and cognition began to emerge (Lave 1988; Rogoff and Lave 1984; Scribner and Cole 1981). Many of the cognitive processes that had been seen as universal and transferable within cognitive psychology were now understood to be closely tied to the particular experimental situation in which they were exercised. It became clear that decontextualised studies of learning could give very misleading results.

A particularly good example is the Adult Math Project in the US, reported in Lave (1988). This research combined traditional testing of mathematical skills with ethnographic observations of the mathematical practices in which people engaged in their everyday lives: for instance, while doing their grocery shopping in the supermarket. It was found that adults performed very differently in experimental settings and in normal everyday activities. Murtaugh (1985) states that, on average, US grocery shoppers scored 59% correct in calculations in decontextualised tests, and 98% correct when shopping in a supermarket. Similar phenomena have been found with Brazilian street children whose ability to perform complex calculations while selling in the streets is not reproduced in 'school maths'-type tests and settings (Nunes *et al* 1993).

This distinction between the results people achieve in tests and the way they deal with real-life problems is brought out by Tennant and Pogson (1995). Drawing on the work of Robert Sternberg (see, for example, Sternberg 1985), they outline common differences between typical test problems and real-life problems. While written test problems are already defined, a key skill in adult life is the ability to define a problem and its parameters in the first place. Test problems usually have a single correct answer, whereas everyday life problems often require people to find a resolution from many different possibilities, none of which is necessarily completely right or wrong. While a test would normally provide all the information necessary to get the right answer, problems in everyday life often have to be resolved without enough information, or on the basis of conflicting pieces of information. Even when decisions have been made, feedback in everyday life is rarely unambiguous. Finally, where test problems are normally required to be solved alone, most of the problems encountered in everyday life are addressed in conjunction with other people. Therefore, the thinking and problem-solving processes in which people engage in everyday situated activity are often very different from the decontextualised cognitive skills addressed by intelligence tests and the like.

This is not to say that transfer between the learning setting and the everyday life setting (where these are separate) is not possible, but it highlights the fact that this is not an unproblematic process. Evans' (2000) research with adults on the relationship between mathematical thinking and emotion develops a model of transfer which acknowledges its complexities. He draws attention to the need for transfer to be seen not as directly carrying over the same 'skill' from one context to another, but as '…a series of reconstructions of ideas and methods from the context of learning, so that they are appropriate for the target setting' (p.232). In addition he claims it is necessary to take account of the often unpredictable influences of affect and emotion, and of the ways in which meanings flow along semiotic chains. He suggests that the ability of a signifier to take on different meanings within different discursive practices provides both the basis of, and limitations on, translation of learning between different practices.

Tennant and Pogson (1995) relate the historically powerful distinction between abstract thought and situated practice to the distinctions made between the theoretical and practical in Western culture, beginning with Greek thinkers such as Plato. 'Practical' intelligence emphasises practice rather than theory, direct usefulness rather than intellectual curiosity, and procedural usefulness rather than declarative knowledge. Everyday action and thought tends to have immediate, visible consequences and a real-life end in mind, which is not the case for 'academic' intelligence.

The authors describe Scribner's 'Milk factory studies' (1983/1997) as an example of this sort of everyday practical reasoning. Scribner combined ethnographic work in an industrial dairy with job simulations and controlled laboratory experiments. The experiments tested hypotheses relating to processes of problem solving and the features distinguishing skilled workers from novices that arose from the ethnographic work. On the basis of this work, she developed a model of 'practical thinking' as a dynamic process embedded in the purposive activities of everyday life, rather than purely as a cognitive construct.

Practical thinking for Scribner has the following characteristics: it is flexible; it is able to solve similar problems in different ways responding to the situation at hand; its problem-solving system is finely tuned to the environment, drawing on social, symbolic and material resources outside the mind of the individual problem-solver; it is driven by principles of economy, with experts designing strategies to save effort wherever possible; it is dependent on knowledge that is specific to the setting (one characteristic of experts was that they used specific dairy- and job-related knowledge to generate flexible and economic procedures); and it is about problem 'formation', that is, reformulating or redefining problems, rather than simply problem 'solving'. Within this model, adult development and adult intelligence must be reconceptualised as comprising practical knowledge and expertise, not cognitive processes alone, and learning is something that happens through sustained engagement in this practice.

Tennant and Pogson go on to explore the implications of several other studies of expertise, knowledge and skill gained through sustained practice and experience, to develop a different way of conceptualising learning. They identify common factors in these studies: experts excel mainly in their own domains; they perceive large meaningful patterns in those domains; they are faster and more economical in what they do; they have superior memory in that particular domain; they see and represent a problem in that domain at a deeper level than novices; they spend a great deal of time analysing a problem qualitatively; and they have strong self-monitoring skills. The authors state that there has been little attempt so far to analyse the implications for adult education of research into expertise.

A significant point made here is that it is important to maintain a distinction between expertise as an outcome, and the acquisition of expertise as a process. It is by initially behaving as novices that experts finally develop expert-type behaviour. Therefore education and training programmes that attempt to teach expertise first may be misguided, if novice-type behaviour is an essential part of the process through which expertise is developed.

Lave and Wenger (1991) studied situated learning in a variety of contexts, developing an understanding of 'learning by doing'. They developed the concept of learning as 'legitimate peripheral participation' in 'communities of practice', as a way of conceptualising the process of development of expertise in practice. They point out that it is possible within a given community for experienced 'old-timers' to engage in the practice that defines the community and, at the same time, for 'novices' to have a legitimate peripheral role, gradually moving into a more central position as they continue to participate in the community's activity.

They examine five ethnographic studies of apprenticeship, looking at the learning processes involved in becoming a Yucatec midwife, a Vai tailor, a naval quartermaster, a supermarket meat cutter and a nondrinking alcoholic. They suggest that the forms of learning in these settings (or failure to learn, particularly in the case of the meat cutters) may be accounted for in terms of the underlying relationships of legitimate peripheral participation in these communities, that is, whether its 'structuring resources' offer the novice possibilities for participating directly in the community's practice.

Wenger (1998) developed the concept of the 'community of practice' in more theoretical detail, defining a community of practice as being a group of people who regularly engage in activity in pursuit of some jointly-negotiated enterprise, thereby developing a shared repertoire of ways of going about things that is constituted in the ongoing process of the community's practice. He refines the notion of learning as participation in practice, and underlines the central role of this participation in the constitution of individual and group identities. This work has been particularly influential within management, with many large companies attempting to promote the development of particular sorts of communities of practice in the workplace.

Other detailed studies of practice in a variety of settings reinforce this perspective on learning in practice. Singleton (1998) is an edited collection of studies from Japan which shows similar processes at work in the way people are trained in traditional arts such as Noh theatre, calligraphy and martial arts, and in everyday socialisation in a variety of Japanese settings. The book 'Understanding Practice' (Chaiklin and Lave 1996) includes studies of a wide variety of activities, from university examinations to maritime navigation. These show how, in each of these settings, learning as situated social practice is ongoing in the community's activities, developing an inherently contextualised understanding of learning to challenge the prevailing decontextualised cognitive models.

The accumulated evidence of this field therefore convinced some to shift from 'a view according to which cognitive processes (and thus learning) are primary and a view according to which social practice is the primary, generative phenomenon, and learning is one of its characteristics' (Lave and Wenger 1991). This means that whenever people engage in social practice, learning will inevitably take place. This is an understanding of learning that moves beyond looking only at changes in people's thought processes, to seeing learning as becoming able to participate in particular sorts of social practices. Learning is understood to be embedded in other forms of social participation, and therefore provision that helps people to engage in social participation is likely to be of more use than provision that aims to equip people with decontextualised skills.

Situated models of learning suggest that we need to understand the sorts of social practices that learners want or need to participate in, and to offer opportunities that enable them to learn through engaging in these practices. More importantly, perhaps, it implies that learners already engage in sophisticated forms of social practice in their everyday lives, in ways that the practices of the classroom may hide. An approach to adult language, literacy and numeracy teaching that acknowledges adults' competence in engaging in practice in their everyday lives, and uses this as a starting-point for education, is a powerful antidote to some prevailing deficit models of adult basic education.

Brain science

Even within the field of brain science, which might seem to be the place where one might most expect to find individual internalised models of human thinking, recent research has demonstrated the socially-situated nature of brain development and the dialectical interpenetration of individual thinking and learning with social context. Early theories in brain science tried to map different areas of the brain to different thought processes, developing concepts such as the idea that the 'right brain' was the location of creativity and the 'left brain' the location of rational processing.

Advances in neuroscience have enabled us to understand more clearly the way the brain is constructed in process, emergent from the interaction between the brain and the environment. Cohen and Leicester (2000) describe how new techniques such as PET and MRI scans have allowed us to develop a better understanding of how the brain works and that, as a result, many neuroscientists have moved on from looking at the brain in terms of specialised areas for particular tasks to seeing it as a network of paths working and combining in parallel. These pathways are continually developed and recombined as people interact with the world around them. The brain is physically formed by this ongoing process of interaction between 'intelligence' and what they call 'extelligence', that is, the cultural capital available in a given context (Stewart and Cohen 1997). Cohen and Leicester suggest that the brain is best understood not in terms of areas reserved for particular sorts of processing, but rather as 'permeable, branching and flexible moving pathways criss-crossing and recursively interacting with each other and with incoming information from the external world (imagine Spaghetti Junction "reeling and writhing" and repeatedly re-assembling).'

This vision of the brain's networks constantly reconstructing themselves through interaction with the world around is similar to the models drawn on by Gee (1992), who develops a model of the mind based on theories of neural networks. Constructors of neural networks have found that artificial neuronal units, arranged in parallel processing networks, can 'learn' to perform tasks simply through a process of trial and error, beginning with a purely random network and 'nudging' it in the direction of increasing accuracy. (The example he gives is of a system developed to distinguish between sonar signals from mines and from rocks.)

Gee suggests that our capacity for learning can be explained in terms of the brain engaging in this sort of ongoing interaction with the world, only in a much more complex way involving recursive interrelationships between many millions of neurons. Again, this is an intrinsically social model of learning, in that the interactions between the neural networks and the world beyond always take place within a socially-constructed world, with the resources drawn on being socially and historically constituted.

In summary, there are two contrasting families of models of learning within psychology. The earlier models, including behaviourism, cognitivism and cognitive constructivism, focused primarily on learning as something that takes place for an individual, whether this learning is seen in terms of changed behaviour patterns or altered mental models and processes. More recently, an alternative paradigm has developed in fields such as sociocultural psychology, social constructivism, activity theory and situated cognition, in which learning is seen as a socially-situated phenomenon, best understood as a feature of people's ongoing participation in social contexts. This second understanding is supported firstly by research that has left the experimental setting and examined the learning processes in people's everyday lives, and secondly by advances in neuroscientific research.

Models from adult education

The review above has examined the principal theories of adult learning developed within various fields of psychology. The discipline of education has also generated a number of models of adult learning, most of which come from within adult education. We begin by considering the theories that attempt to define the distinctive characteristics of adults as learners. We briefly outline the humanistic psychologies on which many of these models draw. We then consider certain elements in models of adult learning that have become particularly influential, including ideas about self-directed learning, learning how to learn, informal learning, reflective and experiential learning and transformative learning. While most of these models come from studies of adult education, we also mention work from research in higher education where this is relevant.

Distinctive characteristics of adult learning

As we have shown above, until the early 1970s most theories of learning came from psychology. Many of these psychological theories of learning are general in nature, often assuming that similar learning processes occur for everybody, whether children or adults. In contrast, theories emerging from the field of adult education have tended to focus more on what is distinctive about adult learning in particular. Coben and Llorente (2003) draw attention to the strengths and weaknesses of this approach. While it has been good to encourage the development of research and theory in the field, it has also closed off some possibilities of dialogue with other fields of social sciences, pedagogy in particular. This has encouraged attention to the differences between working with adults and working with children, rather than to the core issue of the purposes and practices of 'education for all'.

In the early 1970s several influential books were produced which argued that there is something particular about the way adults learn, and that research and practice in adult education should reflect these particularities. These included Houle's 'The Design of Education' (1972), Kidd's 'How Adults Learn' (1978), and perhaps most influentially Knowles' 'The Adult Learner: A Neglected Species' (Knowles 1973; Knowles *et al* 1998).

Knowles outlined a model of adult learning that he called 'andragogy', which consists primarily of a set of assumptions about the adult learner. Knowles claimed that adults have to know why they need to learn something before they undertake to learn it. They must move from a dependent self-concept to a self-directing one. They have accumulated more experience, and experiences of a different quality, than children and their readiness to learn is linked to the tasks associated with their social role and stage of life. Adults engage in problem-centred, rather than subject-centred learning and are driven by internal rather than external motivation.

In the pedagogical model, which Knowles identifies as having been linked historically with teacher-directed education of children, these assumptions are reversed. This model assumes that learners need to know only that they must learn what the teacher teaches and their personality becomes dependent, rather than self-directing. Their own experience is positioned as being of little worth, the experience that counts in the classroom being that of the teacher. They learn what the teacher tells them they need to learn, not what is relevant to their own lives. They are understood to have a subject-centred orientation to learning, and they are seen as being best persuaded to learn through the use of external forms of motivation.

Early editions of Knowles' work make a clear distinction between pedagogy as suitable for children and andragogy as suitable for adults. However, he later came to recognise that different models of teaching and learning are appropriate for different situations. A pedagogical strategy rather than an andragogical one may be most appropriate in some contexts, such as when learners are completely new to a particular subject area (Knowles 1980). However, he claims that the andragogue will only use pedagogical strategies as a first step, and will do everything possible to make the learner themselves responsible for their own learning. He abstracts principles of teaching from these theories of learning.

The implications of the theory of andragogy are that we need to know why people are engaged in learning and make the reasons why we are teaching particular things, in particular ways, explicit. We should support the development of self-direction in learners, be ready to draw on their own experiences where possible, and be aware of the tasks they are engaged in outside the learning environment and the social roles and stages these are associated with. We should relate learning to genuine problems and issues in people's lives, rather than just focusing on decontextualised topics and skills, and we should understand and respect people's own motivations for learning.

Humanistic psychology

Underlying Knowles' model (and many of the other models of adult learning that focus on self-transformation and self-development) are humanistic theories of personal development, such as those of Rogers (Rogers and Freiberg 1994) and Maslow (1970). Humanistic psychology takes human potential and desire for growth as a basic assumption, and sees people as having unlimited potential to improve themselves and seek fulfilment. Maslow and Rogers both assume that people have an intrinsic drive towards growth and self-direction.

Rogers developed his ideas on the basis of years of dealing with clients in therapy. His theory is built around the idea that there is a single force of life known as the 'actualising tendency': a built-in motivation, present in every life form, to make the very best of their existence. He developed a client-centred approach to therapy based on avoiding directiveness and helping the client to reflect on their experiences.

In 'Freedom to Learn', he transferred these person-centred understandings to educational situations. Rogers saw learning as a process initiated by the learner, with the teacher (if there is one) acting simply as a facilitator. The teacher's principal role is to create a secure environment in which learning becomes possible, by developing a relationship with the learner in which the learner's own exploration of themselves and encounter with others is fostered.

Maslow's work developed a model of human development in which there is a hierarchy of needs, the most basic being physiological, followed by needs for love and belonging, and self-esteem. Each of the basic needs must be fulfilled before the next need in the hierarchy becomes salient. At the top of the hierarchy is the need for self-actualisation. When all the previous needs have been satisfied, Maslow suggests that people will naturally turn to learning for self-actualisation.

Models of adult learning from humanistic psychology imply that people have an intrinsic drive for self-development and that this can and should be fostered in education. Another significant implication of these models, particularly in the context of adult language, literacy and numeracy provision, is that people's more basic needs have to be ful-

filled before learning can take place. Someone who is hungry, thirsty, sleepy or ill, feeling excluded, or feeling unsafe is unlikely to learn effectively, because these needs will take priority. It therefore becomes an essential part of the learning process to address issues of this nature. This is especially important given that many learners in the field of adult basic skills live in conditions of social difficulty, many have health problems, and many have had negative experiences of school and other forms of prior learning which can cause them to feel unsafe in any formal learning environment.

Critiques of andragogy

Although the theory of andragogy has been widely taken up, it has also been criticised (Brookfield 1994; Edwards *et al* 995), often on the basis that it is less a theory of adult learning than an ideal state for adult learners to be in – a prescriptive, rather than a descriptive model. People have also questioned whether this model is really a description of the specific characteristics of adult learning, or is merely specific to the types of situations that adult learners tend to be in. This would suggest that it may also apply to some forms of children's learning. The model as it stands largely ignores the significance of the context in which the adult learning takes place. Merriam and Caffarella (1998) cite a variety of empirical studies that have attempted to test the theory, with very mixed results.

Hanson (1996) asks whether there is any need for a separate theory of adult learning at all. She argues that there is little real evidence for an absolute difference between adults and children in terms of their learning. The differences that many theorists believe accumulate with increased age and increased experience may not be as significant as the theory of andragogy assumes. Rather than having a generalised theory of adult learning, based on unsubstantiated, culturally-specific, abstract individualist assumptions about what all adults have in common, she calls for analysis of individuals' own particular characteristics, of the settings and social contexts within which they learn and of their relationships with peers and tutors. She claims that these all contribute to the learning process in specific ways and that:

All-embracing theories only get in the way of developing an understanding of the differing strategies necessary to enable diverse adults to learn different things in different settings in different ways. There are differences, but they are not based on the difference between children and adults, of pedagogy and andragogy. They are differences of context, culture and power. (p.107)

The principal difference in context, culture and power between child learning and adult learning remains that adult learning is usually voluntary, although this is changing in certain settings, for instance where provision of welfare benefits has been linked to compulsory basic skills education. This means that adults normally engage in formal provision in response to needs and wants that they experience in their own lives, rather than because they are following an external directive.

However, most adults engaging in learning in Britain will have experienced compulsory education at some point, the majority for many years. They therefore have a set of memories and associations with learning that they will bring to their experiences of learning in adulthood. While experience clearly serves as a significant basis for learning in adulthood, many adults entering basic skills provision have some negative elements in their previous experiences of learning (Calder 1993). This means that we must take into account not only the factors that pull people towards learning (the reasons why people choose to engage in it), but also the prior associations that may push them away from learning.

Adults are also likely to have other things going on in their lives that can affect their experience of learning. We must not overlook practical issues such as time, money and childcare, all of which need to be addressed if people are to engage with provision.

Brookfield (2000) suggests one possible resolution of this which acknowledges the value of the concept of 'lifelong learning' (seeing learning as a continuum throughout the lifespan), but also takes into account the distinctiveness of learning in adult life in modern Western cultures. Although it is misleading to see adulthood as a completely separate time of life, there are some capacities that appear to be more visible in adult learners in contemporary society. These include the ability to think dialectically and contextually, moving back and forth between general and particular, objective and subjective; the ability to employ practical logic, reasoning within a particular situation in a way that springs from a deep understanding of the context of the situation and pays attention to its internal features; and an ability to become aware of how we know what we know and 'learn to learn'.

Brookfield argues (like Mezirow, see below) that the ability to be critically reflective is only developed as adults pass through experiences of breadth, depth, diversity and differential intensity, over a long period of time. This makes possible critical reflection on the assumptions, beliefs and values assimilated during childhood and adolescence, and assessment of the accuracy and validity of those norms for the contexts of adult life.

A similar perspective is expressed by Coben, FitzSimons and O'Donoghue in the introduction to their work on adults learning mathematics, with specific regard to numeracy (Coben et al. 2000). They claim that the work presented in this volume demonstrates clearly that numeracy is not a decontextualised skill, and that it is not possible to separate the numeracy aspects of everyday activities from the general purposes, goals and social dimensions of action. Therefore, numeracy can be learned and developed only in specific contexts.

> *More recent work on adult learning argues against seeing adults as intrinsically special or different, and in favour of developing more complex understandings of the contextual and cultural assumptions this is based on. Adult learning takes place in specific social contexts, and is engaged in for specific purposes. The way learning develops is directly related to the combination of factors in these specific settings and purposes. Therefore there may not be a singular 'right' model of adult learning that can be applied in teaching. The important thing is to understand the particularities of the contexts and practices in which adult learners are engaged.*

Certain elements of the andragogy model have been taken up and developed in depth, and have become influential concepts within adult education research. We will now move on to describe and assess the contributions of writers who have focused on the elements of self-directed learning, learning how to learn, informal learning, reflective and experiential learning, and transformative learning.

Self-directed learning

The concept of 'self-directed learning' has been represented both in a descriptive way (as another way in which adults are distinctive) and prescriptively (as something which should be encouraged in adult learning provision). It first gained currency with Tough's (1979) studies of adult learning projects in which, through interviews with a wide variety of people, Tough discovered that most adults had engaged in a specific learning project in the previous year, even though most had not been engaged in any formal education.

Since then, the concept has proliferated and is often encountered in adult education literature, used in many different ways. Brockett and Hiemstra (1991) offer one attempt to make sense of the field. They draw attention to the confusion that has surrounded the term, and suggest that it is necessary to distinguish between self-direction as an instructional method, and self-direction as a dimension of personality. Surveying the existing empirical research in the field, they conclude that self-directed learning is not an unusual phenomenon, but a way of life that cuts across socio-economic strata, including supposedly 'hard-to-reach' groups who do not engage readily with formal learning provision.

Any relationship between self-direction in learning and particular demographic variables remains undiscovered, but Brockett and Hiemstra claim that there seems to be a link between self-direction and positive self-concept, and more tentatively between self-direction and life satisfaction. They suggest strategies for enhancing self-direction, which include facilitating critical reflection through reading and writing, promoting rational thinking, and developing people's 'helping skills'. Their understandings are rooted in a humanistic self-development model.

Candy (1991) provides another comprehensive survey of the field. He demonstrates how the concept of self-direction is actually used to gloss at least four distinct concepts. Two of these are activities: autodidaxy, the independent pursuit of learning outside of formal institutional structures; and learner-control, as a way of organising instruction. Two are personal attributes or characteristics: autonomy, as a personal quality or attribute; and self-management in learning, the manifestation of independence of mind or purpose in learning situations.

There are complex relationships between these concepts, and often some conceptual slippage between them. For instance, learner-control in an instructional domain is different from autodidaxy outside formal education. Autonomy in learning does not necessarily give rise to general personal autonomy, nor vice versa. The concepts are also complex in their own right. Autonomy has both a personal and a situational dimension – people who are autonomous in some settings can become very dependent in others, or while dealing with some areas of work rather than others. Most research on autonomy in learning has tended to focus on self-management skills or qualities of personal autonomy, at the expense of the dimension of the learner's construction of the situation. Candy calls for alternative methods of research that see learning as a search for meaning and coherence in one's life, rather than as the acquisition of quantities of information. Thus the emphasis is on the personal significance of the learning to the learner, rather than on 'how much' is learned. He also argues that it is necessary to place the discussion about self-direction into a broader and less individualistic framework. He suggests that interpretive approaches often exaggerate the extent to which the individual's intentions influence the actions they engage in, and underestimate the power of social and cultural factors, such as structures of class, gender, ethnicity and age, to limit people's freedom and choices.

Candy claims that there are important constraints on the extent to which people can or should strive to be self-directed, especially when learning formal or technical bodies of knowledge, as opposed to acquiring greater self-knowledge. He points out that you cannot simply 'graft on' self-directedness in instruction to an education system that is antipathetic to that goal. Approaches to the development of self-directed learning must be congruent with the underlying assumptions of the model which means, among other things, honouring the right of learners to be self-directed with regard to their own self-directedness. It is therefore not necessarily adequate simply to apply learning methods that emphasise learner-control.

This shift to a less individualistic understanding of self-directedness in learning is taken a step further by Collins' (1988) meta-analysis of research and theory in adult learning, which raises questions about the political dimension of the concept, and Hammond and Collins' (1991) account of a course for rural health workers in South Africa which sought to facilitate self-directed learning as a critical practice. For them, this meant a form of learning that started from the assumption that the purpose of education was the betterment of society, and allowed learners to meet their individual learning needs in a way that was informed and guided by a critical analysis of prevailing social needs. This approach saw critical awareness and social action to promote emancipation as desirable results of any educational intervention. Self-directed learning was seen as a way to empower learners to use their learning to improve the conditions under which they lived and worked.

Within adult language, literacy and numeracy, work on self-directed learning implies we should remember that learners have their own motivations for engaging in provision, and are capable of (and probably have a history of) engaging in self-directed autonomous learning. We should therefore respect the autonomy and self-directedness of the learner and see this as a resource to be drawn on in the classroom. We also need to be aware that self-directedness arises from the interaction between an individual and the broader social context in which they engage. We must be conscious of the possibilities for self-directedness that adult learners experience within current structures of provision, and also of any constraints there may be upon it.

Learning how to learn

One outcome of the focus on self-directed learning has been the development of the idea that adults can and should become aware of their own learning processes and how to manage them. 'Learning how to learn' is a concept that has become increasingly popular, particularly with the advent of policies encouraging lifelong learning. The trailblazer in this field was Smith (1983; 1990). His basic point was that adults benefit from actively learning about the cognitive processes thought to be involved in learning, so that they can put them into practice. His book, 'Learning How to Learn: Applied Learning Theory for Adults' (Smith 1983), combined explicit description of a theory of learning with practical guidelines for putting learning how to learn into application in a variety of different settings. These included self-education, group learning projects, learning within educational institutions, learning systematically through reflection on everyday experience, and even learning through intuition and dreams.

Smith suggests that there are four distinctive characteristics of adult learners. Firstly, they have a different orientation to learning from children, since they choose for themselves to engage in education and therefore value time spent in learning. Secondly, they have an accumulation of experience that forms the basis for new learning, and this sum of experience becomes increasingly idiosyncratic as people get older because of the unique nature of each person's path through life. Thirdly, different developmental tasks await adults at different points in their lives, and education is sought during periods of transition. Finally, adult learning is often characterised by anxiety and ambivalence related to negative experiences of early schooling, the contradictory status of being both an autonomous adult and a dependent student, and other similar emotional challenges. Central to the theory of learning underlying his work is the intensely personal nature of the learning process, and the demonstrated capacity of adults to assume partial or total responsibility for educating themselves.

Elements from many of the models described above can therefore be found underlying Smith's work. His distinctive contribution is to suggest that it is in developing an explicit understanding of these models (including, for example, becoming aware of one's preferred learning style) that adults can learn how to learn and become autonomous learners. Since the publication of the first book he has gone on to lead empirical research in the field of learning how to learn (see, for example, Smith 1987; 1990).

Work on learning how to learn implies that adult learning provision should not merely focus on delivering learning or skills, but also needs to include space for discussion and reflection on learners' experiences of their learning, how they learn best, and what they can do to gain more control over and improve their own learning.

Informal learning

There is some overlap between the literature on self-directed learning and that on 'informal learning', a term that has come into favour in recent years. As with self-directed learning, the term has been used in a variety of ways: to describe the way adults learn outside formal provision; to refer to unplanned or unpremeditated learning, or learning which has not been formally structured; to refer to provision in the community as opposed to that which is provided by formal educational institutions; or to refer to any non-accredited provision. This makes a synthesis of the field of informal learning as a whole very difficult. However, it is clear that much of the research examining the way people learn over the course of their lives has brought to light the crucial importance of some form of informal learning in adults' lives, and that this has often been overlooked in favour of work that situates learning primarily within formal provision.

Coffield's (2000) report on the ESRC's 'The Learning Society: Knowledge and Skills for Employment' programme is powerfully entitled, 'The Necessity of Informal Learning'. He underlines the importance of informal learning in the formation of knowledge and skills, describing formal learning in institutions as being merely 'the tip of the iceberg'. The research programme discovered that informal learning is often necessary to do the job, while formal learning is often dispensable. Coffield calls for a profound change in the thinking of government, employers, practitioners and researchers to reflect this insight.

This assessment of the significance of informal learning in adults' lives has been reinforced by a nationwide Canadian telephone survey (Livingstone 2000) which found that over 95% of adults were involved in some form of informal learning activity which they thought of as being significant.

McGivney (1999), in a DfEE study exploring the role of community-based informal learning in widening participation, found that this sort of learning has wide-ranging benefits. It can start people on a path towards more formal, structured or accredited learning provision, and it provides other benefits such as increased confidence, self-esteem, improved personal and social skills, greater autonomy and community regeneration. Similarly, Foley's (1999) work shows the close link between learning and a commitment to transform power relations, through an account of the various forms of incidental learning that can take place when people become involved in social struggle and political activity.

Work on informal learning implies that we need to be aware that learn-ers engage in learning outside the classroom as well as within provision. It suggests that the relation of provision to this other learning should be considered. Research on the amount of unplanned or incidental learning in a variety of settings also suggests that much of the learning taking place even within a formal classroom is not under the teacher's control. Recognising this as something valuable, rather than as some-thing to be avoided, is an important step.

Reflective and experiential models

Adult learning has also been said to be distinctive in that experience, and reflection on this experience, has a central role to play in the process. Each adult life is an accumulation of a unique set of experiences and contexts. Many theories of adult learning developed within adult education look at the significance of this experience for learning.

Dewey's philosophical work underlies much of the literature on reflective and experiential learning. He was interested in the theory of knowledge, and particularly in the application of his theory of inquiry to education. His book, 'How We Think' (1933), originally written for teachers, looked at the relation-ship between reflective thinking and education. His pragmatic epistemology saw reflective thinking as being essentially about real-world problem solving. Encountering a problem, issue or dilemma in the real world sparked a process of reflective thinking, and therefore of learning.

He identified five stages of thinking involved in the process of moving from an initial state of confusion to a final cleared-up, unified, resolved situation:

(1) suggestions, *in which the mind leaps forward to a possible solution; (2) an intellectualization of the difficulty or perplexity that has been* felt *(directly experienced) into a* problem *to be solved, a question for which the answer must be sought; (3) the use of one suggestion after another as a leading idea, or* hypothesis, *to initiate and guide observa-tion and other operations in collection of factual material; (4) the mental elaboration of the idea or supposition as an idea or supposition (reasoning, in the sense in which reasoning is a part, not the whole, of inference); and (5) testing the hypothesis by overt or imaginative action.* (p.107)

Despite the apparent neatness of this list, it is crucial to understand that these stages are not presented as a recipe or algorithm to be followed slavishly. He describes the process of reflective thinking as dynamic, 'messy', and full of false starts and wrong turnings. He makes the important point that the eventual logical form of the solution is the end of a process, rather than a starting-point. The logical product can neither be predicted nor attained without engaging in the messiness of the process. Therefore the fostering of reflective thought does not come in teaching logical form or structure, but in encouraging the pondering of real issues and problems. It is through this process of thinking, making connections, and having the clear gradually emerge from the unclear that concepts and ideas are formed and that learning happens.

In more recent years, Kolb's has been the name most closely associated with reflective and experiential learning. His 'Experiential Learning: Experience as the Source of Learning and Development' (1984) is framed as a 'systematic statement' of the theory of adult learning and its applications to education, work and adult development. Drawing centrally on the work of Lewin, Dewey and Piaget, and reviewing other contributions to the field, Kolb proposes a model of the underlying structure of experiential learning as a continual process of experience of and adaptation to the world, rather than as a series of outcomes.

This process is conceptualised as a cycle that requires the resolution of four conflicting modes of adaptation to the world: concrete experience, reflective observation, abstract conceptualisation and active experimentation. He suggests that the way in which conflicts between these modes are resolved determines the level of learning that results and that, for higher levels of learning, they need to be integrated into a creative synthesis. Learning is thereby defined as a holistic process of adaptation to the world, as well as a process of creating knowledge as the learner interacts with the environment. 'Learning is the process whereby knowledge is created through the transformation of experience.' (Kolb 1984)

Kolb's well-known theory of learning styles comes out of this idea of a four-stage cycle. He suggests that four different learning styles are associated with the four different parts of this cycle. Ideally the learner would draw on different styles at different moments in the cycle, but the uniqueness of each individual's experience means that different people have often acquired different distributions of the four learning styles.

Many see reflection as the crucial element in Kolb's cycle. Brookfield (1994) writes that critical reflection is the 'idea of the decade' for educators looking to prove the uniqueness of adult learning. They take evidence from developmental psychology to claim that it is only adults who are capable of this type of thinking, involving questioning, reframing or replacing existing assumptions, taking alternative perspectives on ideas that were previously taken for

granted, and potentially coming to recognise the hegemonic aspects of dominant cultural values. Boud, Keogh and Walker (1985) also see reflection as
the part of Kolb's cycle that is most important in turning experience into learning. This volume brings together articles that address the role of reflection in
learning in different ways, within a framework that stresses the need to take
time out for active reflection so that learning can come out of experience.

Kolb's work, and particularly the idea of different learning styles, also underlies a great deal of contemporary 'learning to learn' practice. Smith's (1983)
work, described above, claims that:

> *A growing body of research now emerges that leaves little doubt that
> there is a sound basis for taking seriously what has come to be called
> learning style – and that style represents a viable component of the
> whole learning how to learn concept.* (p. 24)

However, much of the work around the concept of learning styles over-simpli-
fies Kolb's analysis. A vast number of different resources and instruments now
exist to help people diagnose their own or their students' learning style and
then to provide teaching to match this, in ways that sometimes make it
appear that a learning style is an essential or fixed trait. Kolb's idea is rather
that the development of each learning style comes in a process of dialectical
adaptation to experience. The 'ideal learner', far from favouring one particular
style, would develop a balance between all four stages in the cycle, and therefore would master all four learning styles as appropriate.

Some have argued that Kolb's own neat four-part distinction is itself based on
an over-simplified model of experience. Miettinen (2000) compares Kolb's
analysis of experience to Dewey's, showing how the subtleties of Dewey's
philosophical approach (which insists, as explained above, on the impos-
sibility of a simple algorithmic approach to reflection) are lost in this four-part
model. Therefore, the idea of identifying one's own or one's students' learning
style and then teaching to this should not be taken up uncritically.

**The work of Dewey and Kolb highlights the central importance to reflec-
tive and experiential learning of finding solutions to real-world
problems. In both of these models, this process involves a variety of
different types of thinking and modes of adaptation to the world. While
the idea of identifying different students' preferred learning styles has
become influential in adult education, for Kolb and Dewey it is the
integration of multiple learning styles or ways of thinking in an ongoing
process that is most important.**

Others who have developed ideas around reflective and experiential learning include Jarvis (1987), whose model of adult learning in social context is based on the idea that learning becomes possible whenever there is a disjuncture between biography and experience. On the basis of interviews and discussions held at a series of workshops with adult educators, he develops a model of learning according to which there are nine potential responses to this disjuncture: three non-learning responses, three non-reflective responses, and three reflective learning responses. This suggests that if there are many different types of learning, no single set of principles for adult learning is likely to cover them all.

The real strength of Jarvis' model is that it allows for the fact that it is the *interaction* between individuals' experience and biography that makes learning possible. If the disjuncture between biography and experience is either too small or too great, then the experience that occurs is more likely to result in meaninglessness than in meaning construction. This interaction will vary from person to person, depending on their particular biography and the particular experiences that they undergo. Thus experience can serve both as a spur and as a barrier to learning, and educators need to try to understand the complexities of learners' biographies, rather than seeing a simple correlation between experience and learning.

Also, given that meaning comes from an interaction between the person and society, a person must be seen as being intrinsically a person-in-society, whose mind and self are themselves socially constructed through this ongoing learning process. He therefore claims that self-development is not necessarily the highest end-product of education. If our aim is for the enhancement of the person-in-society, then education needs to seek to develop both the individual and the social good.

Tennant and Pogson (1995) examine the various ways in which adult educators have attempted to incorporate experience into learning. The justification for the centrality of experience within adult education practices comes from a variety of work: Kolb and Dewey, as described above; Freire's critical literacy, addressed below; the social and cognitive constructivists, such as Piaget and Bruner, who stress the interactive nature of the relationship between learning and experience; and Rogers' and Maslow's stress on the emotionally laden nature of the relationship between experience and learning. They point out that in order for learning to occur, the learner must in some way go beyond experience alone. Instead, experience must be mediated, reconstructed or transformed in some way. They therefore ask the crucial question, how and under what conditions can people reconstruct their experience and thereby learn from it?

They identify four approaches to experiential learning: linking material to prior experiences; relating learning to current experiences; creating new experiences from which to learn, through techniques such as role play and simulation; and learning from lived experience through talking about, analysing, and acting on the implications of that experience, as encouraged by writers on critical reflection like Schön (1983), Boud and associates (1985), and Brookfield (Brookfield 1986; 1987; 1991). They highlight the social and cultural nature of this process of interpretation of experience, seeing self-construction as an ongoing process where the self is in a dialectical relationship with experience, that is to say both forming it and being formed by it.

Reflecting the significance of experience in shaping people's approaches to learning, a number of researchers have employed methods from fields such as oral history and life history to address the significance of adults' prior life experiences and self-concepts in their current learning. Johnston's 'memory work' (2002) around women's memories of mathematics in their lives offers suggestive accounts of the multiple emotional investments and conflicts that have shaped women's attitudes towards the subject. West (1996) studied the motivations of mature students in higher education, using a psychoanalytical-ly-influenced life history approach. His work shows the complexity of adults' motivations for engaging in learning, which had more to do with re-shaping lives, identities and selves than simple economic or vocational purposes. These and other similar studies have brought to light the multi-faceted role of experience in shaping people's learning, both in a positive and in a negative way.

There are many implications of the work on reflective and experiential learning. In all of these models, reflection arises from a problem or an issue people encounter in their real lives, so again we see an insistence on the essentially contextualised nature of adult learning. Provision therefore needs to be related to the real issues that arise for people and lead them to engage in learning in the first place. It is also important to recognise the cyclical nature of this reflective process, and the fact that there are not necessarily any simple algorithms or systems that can be followed to ensure a successful reflection takes place. Each person's process of reflective learning will be based on and driven by the complexities of their own experience, and will therefore be unique to them.

Transformative learning

Critical reflection on experience is central to those models that focus particularly on the transformative potential of adult learning. These theories see learning primarily as a means of personal or social transformation.

Mezirow is the theorist most closely associated with personal transformational models of learning through his model of learning as 'perspective transformation' (Mezirow 1981; 1990; 1991). He outlines his thinking in the first chapter of the 1990 book, a chapter entitled, 'How critical reflection triggers transformative learning'. He suggests that reflection has three primary purposes: to guide action, to give coherence to the unfamiliar, and to reassess the justification of what is already known. It is this third purpose that is central to critical reflection, and works to examine and potentially transform the structure of assumptions within which we make meaning. This structure of assumptions is acquired through socialisation processes, and Mezirow suggests that in adulthood we reassess the assumptions that we acquired during our formative childhood years, often in response to disorienting dilemmas that challenge the notions of reality we had previously taken for granted.

There is a value-judgement associated with the end-goal of 'critical reflection'. Mezirow states clearly (1990:14) that 'more inclusive, discriminating, permeable and integrative perspectives are superior perspectives', and therefore implies that the goal of adult learning is to develop these superior perspectives through processes of critical reflection, leading to perspective transformation.

This is an approach heavily influenced by the humanistic psychological models described earlier. Mezirow's work has been criticised for being too focused on the individual, and for not taking into account the social and cultural factors that govern whether transformation can be possible (Clark and Wilson 1991; Collard and Law 1989). An alternative model of transformative learning is to be found in the work of the Brazilian literacy educator Paulo Freire, which sees learning as central to transformation at the social level (Freire 1972).

Freire's 'pedagogy of the oppressed' was developed through work with the poor and socially excluded in Brazil. He believed the role of education was to liberate people from systematic oppression, and developed a method that taught literacy not as a set of decontextualised skills but as a means of political participation and action.

Freirean methodologies start from people's lived experience, eliciting and working with words and concepts that are already familiar to people in their everyday lives. Education is not seen as something which the teacher brings along and deposits in the students – the 'banking' image of education – which Freire argues merely perpetuates the structures of oppression that have led to social exclusion in the first place. Instead, the teacher is expected to transcend the divide between themselves and the students by committing 'class suicide' as an educator and being reborn (through an 'Easter experience') as a joint educator/educatee with the students (Taylor 1993).

This rebirth is what enables all the people participating in the experience to engage in a real process of dialogue, beginning by discussing their initial words and concepts and drawing out the connections and broader meanings within which they are situated. It is through this dialogue that people develop both literacy and an awareness of the broader structural relations of power and inequality that have led to their social exclusion. Freire calls this awareness *'conscientização'*. In his work, this term implies not merely 'conscientisation' in the sense of awareness, but also praxis – that is, acting to make a real difference in the world. The goal of such 'problem-posing' education is to engage teachers and students in directly addressing these problems in ongoing liberatory action.

Freire's work has been criticised on a variety of fronts (see Taylor 1993). His writing can be dense and unclear, and verges in many places on the mystical. It is not certain how far Freirean literacy programmes in reality actually start from words and concepts that are central to learners' everyday lives, and to what extent they impose their own agendas. Although his programmes, and those inspired by his work, engaged many thousands in literacy education in Brazil and throughout the world, it is difficult to find evidence of Freirean programmes that were directly responsible for achieving significant social change. However, his influence on the development of popular education, literacy education and adult education has been widespread and profound (see Coben 1998 for a thorough assessment of his contribution), and he is one of the principal inspirations behind the radical and critical tradition of adult education.

Taking transformative models of adult learning seriously draws our attention to the potential role of language, literacy and numeracy learning, and adult learning more generally, in both personal and social change.

Postmodern perspectives

Postmodern and poststructuralist thought have been among the main strands in social theory generally in recent years, but few have taken up these ideas within adult learning. Rather than attempting to develop a unified model of adult learning, the postmodern approach pays attention to diversity and fragmentation, seeing the attainment of a single narrative explaining any phenomenon as a way of imposing power that aims to silence dissenting voices, rather than as a representation of truth.

Usher, Bryant and Johnston's 'Adult Education and the Post-Modern Challenge' (1997) disputes the notion of critical reflection on experience as getting closer to 'truth' or to more integrated perspectives, and the notion that higher perspectives can be achieved by perspective transformation, as Mezirow suggests. They demonstrate that experience is always an open text, and that the meaning of experience can never be closed down by critical reflection. Instead, meaning continues to be explored, constructed and reconstructed differently, in an endlessly creative way.

This is a helpful corrective to those models that seek to impose a single model of reflection or learning on what is clearly a very complex process. However, these understandings can be misleading, in that their focus on fragmentation and multiplicity can exclude the patterns that do emerge from the complexity of adult learning interactions, and the ways in which different factors both reproduce and change the regular patterns and meanings of social life. While there may not be any single grand narrative that explains all the social processes involved, there are still real and tangible outcomes of adult learning in terms of encounters that can be described more or less accurately, meanings that people construct for themselves, and changes that people experience.

While it is undoubtedly true that these changes are unstable and shift according to the context within which people find themselves, they are still experienced as real and significant by the people involved, and still have material and social consequences. Something that changes over time in dialectical process is not necessarily completely 'open'. The choice is not between learning as fixed or learning as open and fragmented, but between learning as product and learning as process.

Most of the models of adult learning developed from within adult education move beyond examinations of learning as a decontextualised process to address questions relating to the meanings of, and motivations for, learning in people's lives. This may be in terms of self-direction, reflection, autonomy, problem-solving or transformation and recalls, from a different perspective, the intrinsically socially-situated nature of learning that emerged from the review of the psychological literature. The key point to take from this is that learning for adults is always related to their real lives, their real problems and their real issues, and that we therefore need to try to understand and make links with these, in order for provision to be meaningful, relevant and effective.

Models of learning in contexts of rapid change

So far, although we have been talking about the central importance of the social and the situational in understanding learning, we have not directly engaged with broader ideas of what is going on in society. But since we argue that adult learning is intrinsically social, we must now consider ideas about notions of what is going on in the social setting in which learning takes place. Although they only gave a partial picture, it is possible that individual-based cumulative theories of learning were adequate for previous societies, because rates of change were slower and the need for learning was less. Now, in a quickly changing world, we all have to learn, all the time, and our theories of adult learning reflect the need for this rapid learning in the contexts in which most of us are engaged. Changing work practices call for new models of understanding (Hochschild 1997; Sennett 1998). The needs of the 'knowledge economy' are widely perceived to include the need to adapt quickly to change through learning (Edwards *et al* 1993). The so-called 'new work order' (Gee *et al* 1996) entails rapidly-shifting communicative practices. In this part of the review we will briefly examine some work in two fields that have directly addressed these changing contexts: management learning, and online and distance learning.

Writers in the field of management learning have engaged directly with the issue of learning in a context of rapid change for some time. Burgoyne and Reynolds (1997) claim that the discipline of management learning started in the mid-1970s as a response to a perceived need for reform in management education, training and development. While the early research in management learning aimed to create a single rational framework for understanding the purposes, processes and effects of management education, training and development, in more recent years much more attention has been paid to the particular dynamics of the different contexts in which these processes are played out.

One important recent idea has been that of the 'learning organisation' which, according to Tight (1996), arises directly from a concern about how organisations can survive in the midst of rapid change. Its precursors were in the work of Argyris and Schön (1978) on encouraging organisational learning through action research, coupled with the concerns about quality and value for money associated with concepts such as total quality management and total quality learning. The idea of the learning organisation applies many of the ideas from lifelong learning to the company situation. It is suggested that by encouraging every employee within an organisation to personally invest in seeking continual learning and improvement of quality, the company will develop a competitive edge and be more likely to succeed. Without encouraging this orientation, companies will struggle to cope with the speed of change in a global marketplace.

Vaill (1996), once again from the field of management learning, argues that the rapid social changes we continually experience mean that we live in a world of 'permanent white water' which requires constant learning. His central thesis is that our imaginative and creative initiatives and responses to the systems in which we live and interact are, in fact, continual learning. He draws on a complex systems model of human social life, suggesting that human systems are sociotechnical ones in which, at millions of operational points, human will and human judgements are exercised. These systems are under stress at a multitude of points, a fact which builds turbulence and instability into the system.

It is therefore not in the nature of human social systems to run smoothly, and any attempt at rational design will inevitably meet with unpredictable, emergent change, or unintended consequences. These permanent white water conditions are full of surprises, tend to produce novel problems, and feature events that are 'messy' and ill-structured, with everything in the system potentially being connected to everything else. He claims that this experience of always doing new things and dealing with new problems requires people in contemporary organisations to be (or to become) extremely effective learners. Vaill critiques what he calls the dominant theory of learning, which he sees as resulting from people's formative experiences of learning in institutions. This dominant theory implies that learning is painful; that learning goals are given to us, and that learning is a means to an end that is not of our own choice; and that the person setting out to learn is less admirable than the person who has completed learning. He claims that these common ideas about learning impede the genuine practice of lifelong learning that he sees as being necessary, as well as resting on profound and far-reaching basic assumptions about the nature of learning of which most educators are unaware.

Learning opportunities in management settings, at workshops or conferences, are often set up to mimic the school system, with some cosmetic alterations. However, the learning that emerges from these situations is not the sort of learning that is appropriate for permanent white water conditions. He proposes that we should instead be aiming to develop 'learning as a way of being', a form of learning that is self-directed, creative, exploratory and inventive, expressive, rewarding in the process (not just when a goal is reached), occurring at the levels of feelings and meanings (as much as ideas and skills), and being deinstitutionalised and genuinely continual. This learning process requires reflexivity about the process of learning, as well as about the content of what is learned.

Rapid technological change has specific implications for adult learning, explored in Lea and Nicoll's 'Distributed Learning: Social and Cultural Approaches to Practice' (Lea and Nicoll 2002). This book addresses the use of both new and old technologies as mediational means in distance learning settings, claiming that the historical distinction between face-to-face and distance learning has disappeared, and exploring the way this changes conceptions of learning. They stress that the changes associated with new technologies are not necessarily predictable, because these new technologies are not used in isolation, but are introduced into specific learning settings with existing social practices associated with them. Therefore, rather than suggesting that there can be any single set of changes in learning associated with new technologies, they underline the need to examine the social and cultural practices surrounding technologies in different learning environments, and to understand the specific changes that technology and distance learning bring to particular places and settings.

Models of adult learning developed within contexts of rapid social change recall the broader socially-situated notions of adult learning that have emerged from examining the education and psychological literature. Since it is not merely business and technology but also society as a whole that is experiencing rapid change, adult education as a whole clearly has a responsibility to foster the sorts of learning that are best suited to dealing with this change.

The work described here would suggest that the best way to do this is to encourage exploratory rather than controlled forms of learning, where the learner is empowered to follow their own interests and desires in the learning process, in ways that relate meaningfully to the practices in which they are engaged.

Summary and conclusions

This review has presented a number of different models of adult learning from a variety of different fields. Behaviourist research demonstrates that one particular sort of performance, that which consists merely of behaviour change, can be trained by breaking down complex chains of behaviour into simpler steps and rewarding learners when they perform each step. Gradually learners approximate more and more closely to the desired behaviour.

However, these approaches cannot address the non-material aspects of learning and understanding that are at the heart of learning. A cognitivist perspective shows that behaviour does not necessarily correlate with understanding, and that we need to find ways to build on people's existing knowledge to help them make sense of new information. Cognitive constructivism brings to light the learner's active role in this process, and the need to support learners in making their own meanings and connections.

Developmental theories add the understanding that people pass through different stages in their lives, in which they take on different social and cultural roles and responsibilities. Provision needs to take account of this and find ways to understand and respond to the sorts of practices and problems people engage with in their lives outside the classroom. At the same time, provision needs to recognise the socially- and culturally-shaped nature of these developmental models, and the implications of the pressures people experience to meet expectations about appropriate choices and behaviour at particular points in their lives. It is important to resist inappropriate models of adult development, particularly those that assume there is a single developmental path and end-point towards which we should all be aiming.

Activity theory and social constructivism draw attention to the central role played by social interaction and by material and symbolic mediational tools in the learning process. This suggests that interaction with the learner, at the level that is right for them, and the use of appropriate mediational tools and strategies, are both necessary for learning. Studies in situated cognition underline the importance of the practices within which learning is located, offering a new understanding of learning as a form of participation in social practice, rather seeing it only in terms of behaviour or cognitive processes. This socially- and historically-constructed model of learning is supported from another field by advances in neuroscience, which give biophysical explanations for our capacity for learning and show how neural networks develop in a process of interaction within a wider social and cultural context.

Moving on to models from the field of adult education, the theory of andragogy suggests that adult learning is distinctive in a variety of ways. Adults are supposed to be self-directed and they need to know why they need to learn something. They have accumulated more and different experiences than children and their learning is linked to their social role and stage or life. They engage in problem-centred rather than subject-centred learning and they are internally, rather than externally, motivated. However, critics of andragogy suggest that taking note of the different contexts and practices in which adults engage is more important than identifying what is intrinsically different about adults.

Work on self-directed learning suggests that this is not merely a desirable property of an individual learner, but arises from a complex set of factors in social interaction. Ideas concerning learning to learn demonstrate that it is useful for adult learners to have space and time to reflect on their learning processes, as well as on the particular topics addressed in class. Research has brought to light the significance of informal and incidental learning in people's lives and implies the need to be aware of adults' learning outside formal provision and to see unplanned learning within the classroom as a resource. The work on reflective and experiential learning shows the significance of real-life problems, situations and issues for people's learning and the uniqueness and unpredictability of each person's process of reflection.

Mezirow's personal transformative model suggests that reflection is crucial to personal transformation, but he does not address social and cultural possibilities for transformation or constraints upon it. Freire's work draws attention to the broader potential role of dialogical approaches to literacy learning for social transformation.

Postmodern and poststructuralist models of adult learning are useful in their attention to questions of fragmentation, diversity and meaning construction in learning. However, there is a difference between seeing learning as a complex evolving process, and understanding it as being completely open. Too much attention to difference and fragmentation in learning can cause us to lose sight of the significant patterns that emerge in people's learning and lives.

Finally, some models have confronted the issue of learning in contexts of rapid social and technological change, particularly in management learning and in online and distance education. These models reinforce the arguments for flexible approaches to learning and provision that engage centrally with the learner's own contexts and practices.

It is clear that it would be partial and misleading to see adult learning only as an individual cognitive phenomenon, or even as something that can be fully controlled by a teacher transmitting particular curriculum content. Instead, learning is present in a dialectical interaction between individual, situational and social factors. The learner's contexts, purposes and practices are the most important factors in the process.

In summary, the inferences drawn from this review are as follows:

1. Adults have their own motivations for learning. Learners build on their existing knowledge and experience. They fit learning into their own purposes and become engaged in it. People's purposes for learning are related to their real lives and the practices and roles they engage in outside the classroom.

2. Adults have a drive towards self-direction and towards becoming autonomous learners. Learning is initiated by the learner and one role of the teacher is to provide a secure environment in which learning can take place.

3. Adults have the ability to learn about their own learning processes, and can benefit from discussion and reflection on this. They are able to learn how to learn. For instance, there are different learning styles that people synthesise. Teaching can enable learners to develop their range of learning styles.

4. Learning is a characteristic of all real-life activities, in which people take on different roles and participate in different ways. People learn by engaging in practice and their participation can be supported in new ways. Teaching can 'scaffold' these activities, enabling learners to develop new forms of expertise.

5. Adults reflect and build upon their experience. Reflective learning is generated when people encounter problems and issues in their real lives and think about ways of resolving them.

6. Reflective learning is unique to each person, since it arises out of the complexities of their own experience. A great deal of learning is incidental and idiosyncratically related to the learner: it cannot be planned in advance. While there are things that can be done to encourage reflective experiential learning, there is no set of steps that can be followed to guarantee it will happen.

7. Reflective learning enables people to reorganise experience and 'see' situations in new ways. In this way, adult learning is potentially transformative, both personally and socially.

References

Argyris, C. and D. Schön (1978). **Organizational learning: a theory of action perspective.** Reading, MA: Addison-Wesley.

Ausubel, D. (1963). **The Psychology of Meaningful Verbal Learning.** New York: Grune & Stratton.

Bandura, A. (1977). Social Learning Theory. Englewood Cliffs, New Jersey: Prentice Hall.

Baxter Magolda, M. (1992). **Knowing and Reasoning in College: Gender-Related Patterns in Students' Intellectual Development.** San Francisco: Jossey-Bass.

Belenky, M. F., B. M. Clinchy, N. R. Goldberger and J. M. Tarule (1986). **Women's Ways of Knowing: The Development of Self, Voice and Mind.** New York: Basic Books.

Boud, D., R. Keogh and D. Walker, Eds. (1985). **Reflection: Turning Experience Into Learning.** London: Kogan Page.

Brockett, R. G. and R. Hiemstra (1991). **Self-direction in Adult Learning: Perspectives on Theory, Research, and Practice.** New York: Routledge.

Brookfield, S. D. (1986). **Understanding and Facilitating Adult Learning.** Buckingham: Open University Press.

— (1987). **Developing Critical Thinkers.** San Francisco: Jossey-Bass.

— (1991). 'The Development of Critical Reflection in Adulthood.' **New Education** 13(1): 39-48.

— (1994). 'Adult Learning: An Overview.' **International Encyclopedia of Education.** A. Tuijnman, Ed. Oxford: Pergamon Press.

— (2000). 'Adult cognition as a dimension of lifelong learning.' **Lifelong Learning: Education Across the Lifespan.** J. Field and M. Leicester, Eds. London: RoutledgeFalmer.

Bruner, J. (1960, 1977). **The Process of Education.** Cambridge, MA: Harvard University Press.

— (1985). 'Vygotsky: a historical and conceptual perspective.' **Culture, Communication and Cognition: Vygotskian Perspectives.** J. V. Wertsch, Ed. Cambridge: Cambridge University Press.

Burgoyne, J. and M. Reynolds (1997). **Management Learning: Integrating Perspectives in Theory and Practice.** London: Thousand Oaks, New Delhi: Sage.

Calder, J. Ed. (1993). **Disaffection and Diversity: Overcoming Barriers for Adult Learners.** London: Falmer.

Candy, P. C. (1991). **Self-direction for Lifelong Learning: A Comprehensive Guide to Theory and Practice.** San Francisco: Jossey-Bass.

Chaiklin, S. and J. Lave (1996). **Understanding Practice: Perspectives on Activity and Context.** Cambridge: Cambridge University Press.

Clark, M. C. and A. L. Wilson (1991). 'Context and Rationality in Mezirow's Theory of Transformational Learning.' **Adult Educational Quarterly** 41(2): 75-91.

Coben, D. (1998). **Radical Heroes: Gramsci, Freire and the Politics of Adult Education.** New York and London: Garland/Taylor and Francis.

Coben, D. and J. C. Llorente (2003). 'Conceptualising education for all in Latin America.' **Compare** 33(1): 101-113.

Coben, D., J. O'Donoghue and G. E. FitzSimons, Eds. (2000). **Perspectives on Adults Learning Mathematics: Research and Practice.** Dordrecht, The Netherlands: Kluwer Academic Publishers.

Coffield, F. Ed. (2000). **The Necessity of Informal Learning.** Bristol: The Policy Press.

Cohen, J. and M. Leicester, (2000). 'The evolution of the learning society: brain science, social science and lifelong learning.' **Lifelong Learning: Education Across the Lifespan.** J. Field and M. Leicester, Eds. London: RoutledgeFalmer.

Cole, M., Y. Engeström, and O. Vasquez, Eds. (1997). **Mind, Culture and Activity: Seminal Papers from the Laboratory of Comparative Human Cognition.** Cambridge: Cambridge University Press.

Collard, S. and M. Law (1989). 'The Limits of Perspective Transformation: A Critique of Mezirow's Theory.' **Adult Educational Quarterly** 39(2): 99-107.

Collins, M. (1988). 'Self-directed Learning or an Emancipatory Practice of Adult Education: Re-thinking the Role of the Adult Educator.' Proceedings of the 29th Annual Adult Education Research Conference, Calgary: Faculty of Continuing Education, University of Calgary.

Dewey, J. (1933). **How We Think: A Restatement of the Relation of Reflective Thinking to the Educative Process.** 2nd edition. New York: D. C. Heath.

Edwards, R., A. Hanson and P. Raggatt, Eds. (1995). **Boundaries of Adult Learning.** London: Routledge.

Edwards, R., S. Sieminski, and D. Zeldin, Eds. (1993). **Adult Learners, Education and Training.** London: Routledge in association with the Open University.

Erikson, E. H. (1963). **Childhood and Society.** 2nd (revd) edition. New York: Norton.

— (1978). **Adulthood.** New York: Norton.

— (1982). **The Lifecycle Completed: A Review.** New York: Norton.

Erikson, E. H., J. M. Erikson and H. O. Kivnick (1986). **Vital Involvement in Old Age.** New York: Norton.

Evans, J. (2000). **Adults' Mathematical Thinking and Emotions.** London and New York: RoutledgeFalmer.

Foley, G. Ed. (1999). **Learning in Social Action: A Contribution to Understanding Informal Education.** Leicester: NIACE.

Freire, P. (1972). **Pedagogy of the Oppressed.** London: Penguin.

Gagné, R. (1985). **The Conditions of Learning and Theory of Instruction.** 4th edition. New York: Holt, Rinehart and Winston.

Gee, J. P. (1992). **The Social Mind: Language, Ideology, and Social Practice.** New York: Bergin & Garvey.

Gee, J. P., G. Hull, and C. Lankshear (1996). **The New Work Order: Behind the Language of the New Capitalism.** St Leonards, NSW: Allen and Unwin.

Hammond, M. and R. Collins (1991). **Self-directed Learning: Critical Practice.** London: Kogan Page.

Hanson, A. (1996). 'The search for a separate theory of adult learning: does anyone really need andragogy?' **Boundaries of Adult Learning.** R. Edwards, A. Hanson and P. Raggatt, Eds. London and New York: Routledge in association with the Open University.

Hochschild, A. (1997). **The Time Bind: When Work becomes Home and Home becomes Work.** New York: Metropolitan Books.

Houle, C. O. (1972). **The Design of Education.** San Francisco: Jossey-Bass.

Jarvis, P. (1987). **Adult Learning in the Social Context.** London: Croom Helm.

Johnston, B. (2002). 'Capturing numeracy practices: memory work and time.' **Ways of Knowing Journal** 2(1): 33-44.

Kidd, J. R. (1978). **How Adults Learn**, Englewood Cliffs: Cambridge/Prentice Hall.

King, P. M. and K. S. Kitchener (1994). **Developing Reflective Judgment**. San Francisco: Jossey-Bass.

Knowles, M. (1973). **The Adult Learner: A Neglected Species**. Houston, TX: Gulf Publishing Company.

— (1980). **The Modern Practice of Adult Education: Andragogy versus Pedagogy.** Revised and updated edition. Chicago: Follett Publishing Company.

Knowles, M., E. F. Holton and R. A. Swanson (1998). **The Adult Learner: The Definitive Classic in Adult Education and Human Resource Development.** 5th edition. Houston, TX: Gulf Publishing Company.

Kohlberg, L. (1981). **Essays on Moral Development vol. 1: The Philosophy of Moral Development: Moral Stages and the Idea of Justice.** San Francisco and London: Harper & Row.

— (1984). **Essays on Moral Development vol. 2: The Psychology of Moral Development: the Nature and Validity of Moral Stages**. San Francisco and London: Harper & Row.

Kolb, D. (1984). **Experiential Learning: Experience as the Source of Learning and Development.** New Jersey: Prentice Hall.

Lave, J. (1988). **Cognition in Practice: Mind, Mathematics and Culture in Everyday Life.** Cambridge: Cambridge University Press.

Lave, J. and E. Wenger (1991). **Situated Learning: Legitimate Peripheral Participation.** Cambridge: Cambridge University Press.

Lea, M. R. and K. Nicoll, Eds. (2002). **Distributed Learning: Social and Cultural Approaches to Practice.** London and New York: RoutledgeFalmer with the Open University.

Leont'ev, A. N. (1978). **Activity, consciousness, and personality.** Englewood Cliffs and London: Prentice Hall.

— (1981). **Problems of the Development of the Mind.** Moscow: Progress Publishers.

Livingstone, D. W. (2000).'Researching Expanded Notions of Learning and Work and Underemployment: Findings of the First Canadian Survey of Informal Learning Practices.' **International Review of Education** 46(6): 491-514.

Luria, A. R. (1976). **Cognitive Development, its Cultural and Social Foundations.** M. Cole, Ed. Cambridge, MA and London: Harvard University Press.

— (1978). **The Selected Writings of A. R. Luria.** M Cole, Ed. White Plains, NY: M. E. Sharpe.

Maslow, A. (1970). **Motivation and Personality.** 2nd edition. New York: Harper and Row.

McGivney, V. (1999). **Informal Learning in the Community: A Trigger for Change and Development.** Leicester: National Institute of Adult Continuing Education.

Merriam, S. B. and R. S. Caffarella (1998). **Learning in Adulthood: A Comprehensive Guide.** 2nd edition. New York: Jossey-Bass.

Merriam, S. B. and M. C. Clark (1991). **Lifelines: Patterns of Work, Love, and Learning in Adulthood.** San Francisco: Jossey-Bass.

Mezirow, J. (1981). 'A Critical Theory of Adult Learning and Education.' **Adult Education** 32(1): 3-24.

— Ed. (1990). **Fostering Critical Reflection in Adulthood**. San Francisco: Jossey-Bass.

— (1991). **Transformative Dimensions of Adult Learning**. San Francisco: Jossey-Bass.

Miettinen, R. (2000). 'The concept of experiential learning and John Dewey's theory of reflective thought and action.' **International Journal of Lifelong Education** 19(1): 54-72.

Miller, N. E. and J. Dollard (1941) **Social Learning and Imitation**. New Haven: Yale University Press.

Murtaugh, M. (1985). 'The practice of arithmetic by American grocery shoppers.' **Anthropology and Education Quarterly** 16: 186-192.

Neugarten, B. (1976). 'Adaptation and the life cycle.' **American Journal of Psychiatry** 136: 887-893.

Nunes, T., A. D. Schliemann, and D. W. Carraher (1993). **Street Mathematics and School Mathematics**. Cambridge: Cambridge University Press.

Perry, W. G. (1970). **Forms of Intellectual and Ethical Development in the College Years.** Austin, TX: Holt, Rinehart & Winston.

Piaget, J. (1950). **Introduction à l'épistémologie génétique.** Paris: Presses Universitaires de France.

— (1970) **The Science of Education and the Psychology of the Child**. New York: Grossman.

Riegel, K. F. (1976). 'The dialectics of human development.' **American Psychologist** 31: 689-700.

Rogers, C. and H. J. Freiberg, (1994). **Freedom to Learn**. 3rd edition. New York: Prentice Hall.

Rogoff, B. and J. Lave (1984). **Everyday Cognition: Its Development in Social Context**. Cambridge, MA: Harvard University Press.

Schön, D. (1983). **The Reflective Practitioner: How Professionals Think in Action.** New York: Basic Books.

Scribner, S. (1983/1997). 'Mind in action: a functional approach to thinking.' **Mind, Culture and Activity: Seminal Papers from the Laboratory of Human *Cognition***. M. Cole, Y. Engeström and O. Vasquez, Eds. Cambridge: Cambridge University Press.

Scribner, S. and M. Cole (1981). **The Psychology of Literacy**, Cambridge, MA: Harvard University Press.

Sennett, R. (1998). **The Corrosion of Character: The Personal Consequences of Work in the New Capitalism**, London and New York: Norton.

Singleton, J. Ed. (1998). **Learning in Likely Places: Varieties of Apprenticeship in Japan.** Cambridge: Cambridge University Press.

Skinner, B. F. (1974). **About Behaviorism.** New York: Random House.

Smith, R. M. (1983). **Learning How to Learn: Applied Learning Theory for Adults.** Milton Keynes: Open University Press.

— Ed. (1987). **Theory Building for Learning How to Learn.** Chicago: Educational Studies Press.

— Ed. (1990). **Learning to Learn Across the Lifespan.** San Francisco: Jossey-Bass.

Sternberg, R. (1985). **Beyond IQ: A Triarchic Theory of Human Intelligence.** Cambridge and New York: Cambridge University Press.

Stewart, I. and J. Cohen (1997). **Figments of Reality.** Cambridge: Cambridge University Press.

Taylor, P. V. (1993). **The Texts of Paulo Freire.** Buckingham: Open University Press.

Tennant, M. and P. Pogson (1995). **Learning and Change in the Adult Years: A Developmental Perspective.** San Francisco: Jossey-Bass.

Tight, M. (1996). **Key Concepts in Adult Education and Training.** London and New York: Routledge.

Tough, A. (1979). **The Adult's Learning Projects: A Fresh Approach to Theory and Practice in Adult Learning.** Toronto: The Ontario Institute for Studies in Education.

Usher, R. S., I. Bryant and R. Johnston (1997). **Adult Education and the Post-Modern Challenge**, London and New York: Routledge.

Vaill, P. B. (1996). **Learning as a Way of Being: Strategies for Survival in a World of Permanent White Water.** San Francisco: Jossey-Bass.

Vygotsky, L. S. (1962). **Thought and Language**, Cambridge, MA: MIT Press.

— (1978). **Mind in Society**. Cambridge, MA: Harvard University Press.

Wenger, E. (1998). **Communities of Practice: Learning, Meaning and Identity.** Cambridge: Cambridge University Press.

Wertsch, J. V. (1985a). **Culture, Communication, and Cognition: Vygotskyan Perspectives.** Cambridge: Cambridge University Press.

(1985b). **Vygotsky and the Social Formation of Mind.** Cambridge, MA: Harvard University Press.

(1991). **Voices of the Mind: A Sociocultural Approach to Mediated Action.** Hemel Hempstead: Harvester Wheatsheaf.

West, L. (1996). **Beyond Fragments: Adults, Motivation and Higher Education - A Biographical Analysis.** Bristol, PA and London: Taylor & Francis.